SCOTT JOPLIN RAGTIME

CLASSICS FOR PIANO DUET

Arranged for One Piano–Four Hands by

DENES AGAY

Contents

EDWARD B. Marks Music Company

EXCLUSIVELY DISTRIBUTED BY

HAL•LEONARD® CORPORATION

GLADIOLUS RAG

Composer's Note:
Do not play this piece fast.
It is never right to play
"Ragtime" fast.

SCOTT JOPLIN
Arranged by Denes Agay

Slow march tempo

Secondo

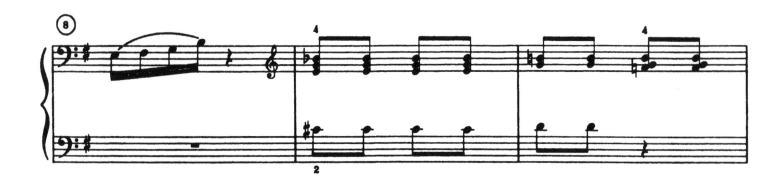

GLADIOLUS RAG

Composer's Note:
Do not play this piece fast.
It is never right to play
"Ragtime" fast.

SCOTT JOPLIN
Arranged by Denes Agay

Slow march tempo

Primo

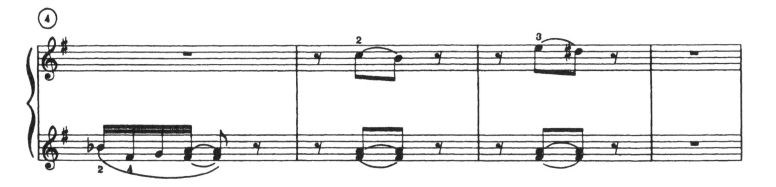

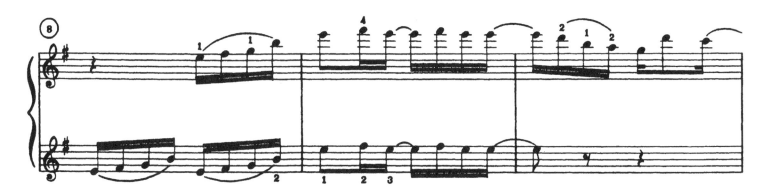

Secondo

4

Secondo

Secondo

MAPLE LEAF RAG

SCOTT JOPLIN
Arranged by Denes Agay

Tempo di Marcia

Secondo

MAPLE LEAF RAG

SCOTT JOPLIN
Arranged by Denes Agay

Secondo

Primo

Secondo

Primo

Secondo

SCOTT JOPLIN'S NEW RAG

SCOTT JOPLIN
Arranged by Denes Agay

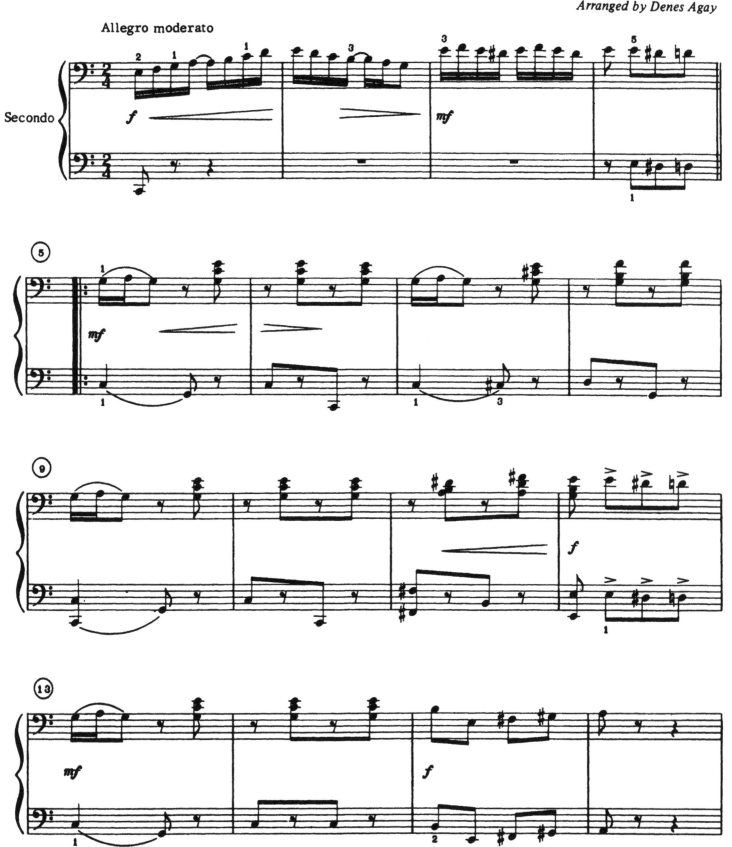

SCOTT JOPLIN'S NEW RAG

SCOTT JOPLIN
Arranged by Denes Agay

Secondo

Secondo

(Melody)

"THE EASY WINNERS"

SCOTT JOPLIN
Arranged by Denes Agay

"THE EASY WINNERS"

SCOTT JOPLIN
Arranged by Denes Agay

Secondo

Primo

"STOPTIME" RAG

SCOTT JOPLIN
Arranged by Denes Agay

* To get the desired effect of "Stoptime" the pianist should stamp the heel of one foot heavily upon the floor on every beat of each measure.

† Composer's own designation.

"STOPTIME" RAG

SCOTT JOPLIN
Arranged by Denes Agay

* To get the desired effect of "Stoptime" the pianist should stamp the heel of one foot heavily upon the floor on every beat of each measure.

† Composer's own designation.

Secondo

THE CASCADES

SCOTT JOPLIN
Arranged by Denes Agay

Tempo di Marcia

Secondo

THE CASCADES

SCOTT JOPLIN
Arranged by Denes Agay

Tempo di Marcia

Primo

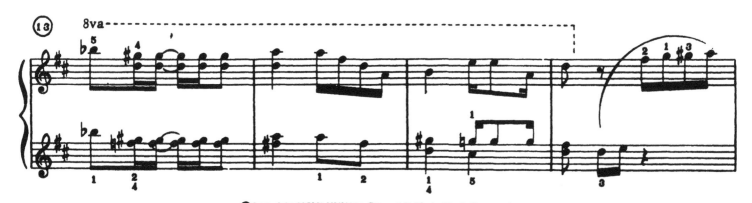

Secondo

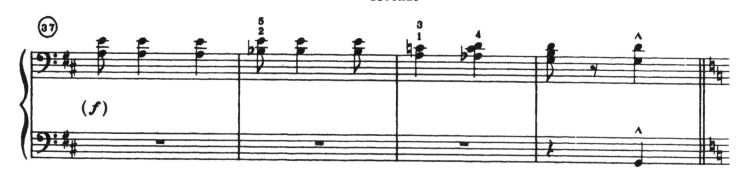

Secondo

THE ENTERTAINER

SCOTT JOPLIN
Arranged by Denes Agay

Secondo

THE ENTERTAINER

SCOTT JOPLIN
Arranged by Denes Agay

Secondo

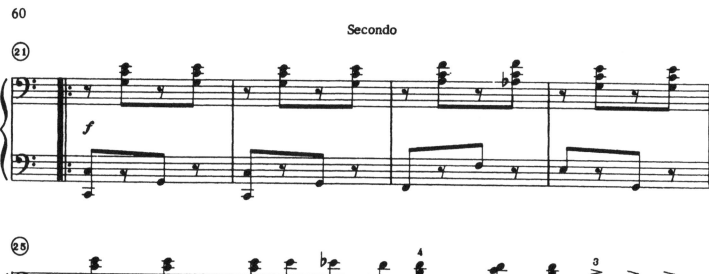

Secondo

64